Contents

About the Sun

The Sun shines.

Feel its heat.

See its light.

The Sun

by Martha E. H. Rustad

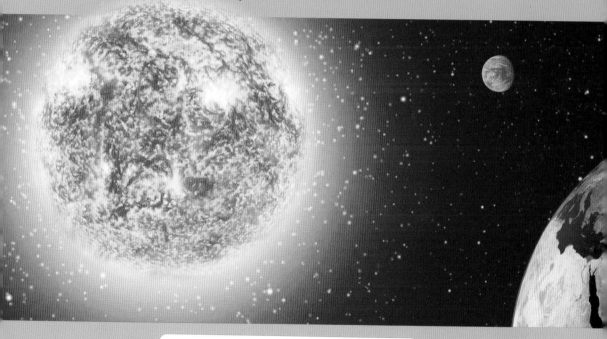

Raintree is an imprint of Capstone Global Library Limited, a company incorporated in England and Wales having its registered office at 264 Banbury Road, Oxford, OX2 7DY – Registered company number: 6695582

www.raintree.co.uk
myorders@raintree.co.uk

Text © Capstone Global Library Limited 2016
The moral rights of the proprietor have been asserted.

Edited by Erika L. Shores
Designed by Juliette Peters and Katelin Plekkenpol
Picture research by Tracy Cummins
Production by Katy LaVigne
Originated by Capstone Global Library

Printed and bound in China.

ISBN 978 1 4747 1252 1 (hardback)

19 18 17 16 15
10 9 8 7 6 5 4 3 2 1

ISBN 978 1 4747 1256 9 (paperback)

20 19 18 17 16
10 9 8 7 6 5 4 3 2 1

British Library Cataloguing in Publication Data
A full catalogue record for this book is available from the British Library.

Acknowledgements
We would like to thank the following for permission to reproduce photographs: Getty Images: Juice Images, 5; Science Source: Eric Cohen, 13, Mark Garlick, 9; Shutterstock: Kalenik Hanna, Design Element, lassedesignen, 19, Mopic, 15, Paul Fleet, 17, PaulPaladin, 11, Triff, Cover, 1, 7, Zurijeta, 21.

Every effort has been made to contact copyright holders of material reproduced in this book. Any omissions will be rectified in subsequent printings if notice is given to the publisher.

Editor's Note
In this book's photographs, the sizes of objects and the distances between them are not to scale.

What is the Sun?

A star!

Stars are balls

of burning gases.

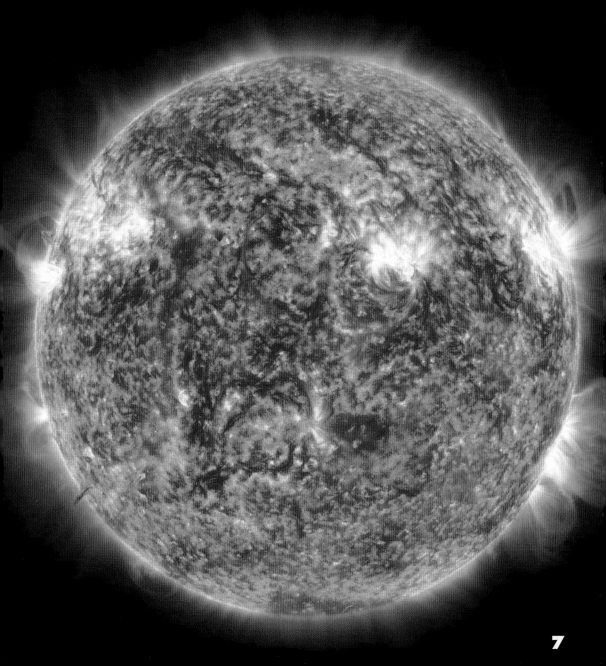

The Sun's place

The Sun sits in the Milky Way. Our galaxy looks like a disc.

Milky Way galaxy

Sun

How far away is the Sun?
About 150 million kilometres
(93 million miles)!

Big and hot

The Sun is huge.

It is as wide as 109 Earths.

Earth

Sun

13

Inside the Sun is the core.

The Sun is hottest there.

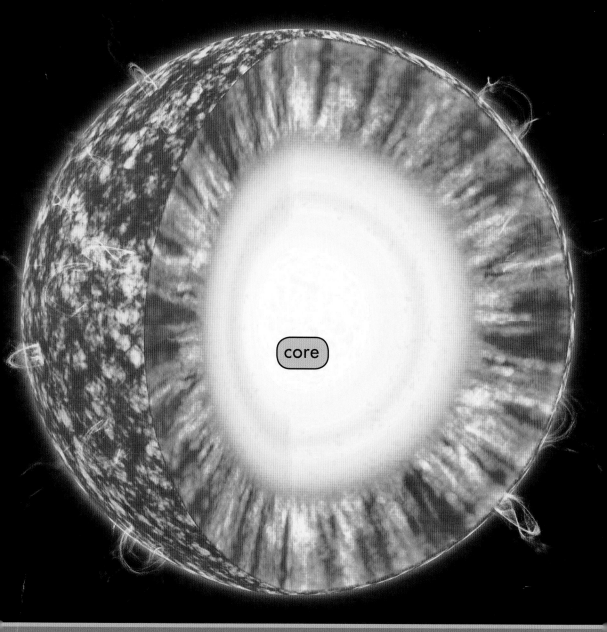

core

Solar flares shoot out.

Hot gases escape.

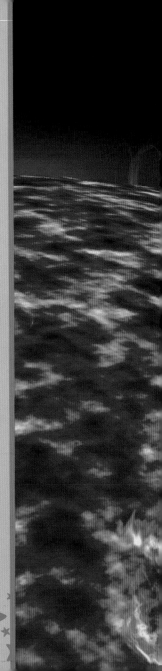

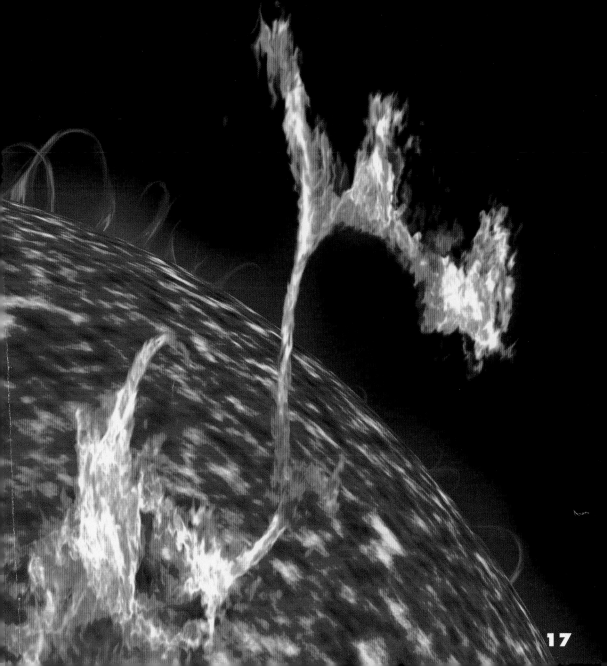

The Sun and Earth

The Sun always shines.

Earth turns. Our side faces

the Sun. It is day.

Our side turns away.

It is night.

We need the Sun.

Its heat warms Earth.

Its rays light Earth.

Thank you, Sun!

Glossary

galaxy large group of billions of stars

gas substance that spreads to fill any space that holds it

planet large object in space that orbits a star

ray line of light and heat

solar flare burst of energy and gas from the Sun's surface

star ball of burning gases; the Sun is a star

Find out more

Sun, Moon and Stars (Kingfisher Readers), Hannah Wilson (Kingfisher, 2014)

The Sun (Space). Charlotte Guillain (Raintree, 2010)

Websites

solarsystem.nasa.gov/planets/profile.cfm?Object=Sun
Learn facts about the Sun on this website.

www.spacecentre.co.uk
Visit the National Space Centre in Leicester.

Index